Group's

BIBLE SENSE™

PHILIPPIANS

//SHARING THE JOY OF JESUS

Group

Loveland, Colorado

www.group.com

Group resources actually work!

This Group resource incorporates our R.E.A.L. approach to ministry. It reinforces a growing friendship with Jesus, encourages long-term learning, and results in life transformation, because it's

Relational
Leaner-to-learner interaction enhances learning and builds Christian friendships.

Experiential
What learners experience through discussion and action sticks with them up to 9 times longer than what they simply hear or read.

Applicable
The aim of Chistian education is to equip learners to be both hearers and doers of God's Word.

Learner-based
Learners understand and retain more when the learning process takes into consideration how they learn best.

Group's BIBLESENSE™

PHILIPPIANS: Sharing the Joy of Jesus
Copyright © 2006 Group Publishing, Inc.

Visit our Web site: **www.group.com**

Credits
Contributors: Keith Madsen, David Trujillo, Kelli B. Trujillo, and Roxanne Wieman
Editor: Carl Simmons
Creative Development Editor: Matt Lockhart
Chief Creative Officer: Joani Schultz
Copy Editor: Amber Van Schooneveld
Art Director: Kari K. Monson
Cover Art Director: Jeff A. Storm
Cover Designer: Andrea Filer
Photographer: Rodney Stewart
Production Manager: DeAnne Lear

Unless otherwise indicated, all Scripture quotations are taken from the *Holy Bible,* New Living Translation, copyright © 1996, 2004. Used by permission of Tyndale House Publishers, Inc., Wheaton, Illinois 60189. All rights reserved.

Library of Congress Cataloging-in-Publication Data
Philippians : sharing the joy of Jesus.
    p. cm. -- (Group's BibleSense)
  Includes bibliographical references.
  ISBN-13: 978-0-7644-3225-5 (pbk. : alk. paper)
  1. Bible. N.T. Philippians--Study and teaching. 2. Bible. N.T. Philippians--Criticism, interpretation, etc. I. Group Publishing. II. Series.
  BS2705.55.P45 2006
  227'.60071--dc22
                                      2006008356
ISBN: 0-7644-3225-7

10 9 8 7 6 5 4 3 2 1   15 14 13 12 11 10 09 08 07 06
Printed in the United States of America.

CONTENTS

TO GROUP'S
BIBLESENSE™

Welcome to **Group's BibleSense™**, a book-of-the-Bible series unlike any you've ever seen! This is a Bible study series in which you will literally be able to *See, Hear, Smell, Taste, and Touch God's Word*—not only through seeing and hearing the actual book of the Bible you're studying on DVD but also through thought-provoking questions and group activities. As you do these sessions, you'll bring the Word to life, bring your group closer together as a community, and help your group members bring that life to others.

Whether you're new to small groups or have been doing them for years, you'll discover new, exciting, and—dare we say it—*fun* ways to learn and apply God's Word to your life in these sessions. And as you dig deeper into the Bible passage for each session and its meaning to your life, you'll find your life (and the lives around you) transformed more and more into Jesus' likeness.

Each session concludes with a series of opportunities on how to commit to reaching your world with the Bible passage you've just studied—whether it's in changing your own responses to others, reaching out to them individually or as an entire group, or by taking part in something bigger than your group.

So again, welcome to the world of BibleSense! We hope you'll find the experiences and studies here both meaningful and memorable and that as you do them together, your lives will grow even more into the likeness of our Lord, Jesus Christ.

—Carl Simmons, Editor

ABOUT THE SESSIONS

TASTE AND SEE (20 minutes)

Every BibleSense session begins with food—to give group members a chance to unwind and transition from a busy day and other preoccupations into the theme of the session. After the food and a few introductory questions, the group gets to experience Scripture in a fresh way. The passage for each session is included on DVD, as well as in print within the book. Also provided is "A Sense of History," a brief feature offering additional cultural and historical context.

DIGGING INTO SCRIPTURE (30 minutes)

This is the central part of the session. The group will have the chance to interact with the Scripture passage you've just read and watched, and, through questions and other sensory experiences, you'll learn how it applies to *your* life.

MAKING IT PERSONAL (15 minutes)

Now you'll move from understanding *how* the passage applies to your life to thinking about ways you *can* apply it. In this part of the session, personal meaning is brought home through meaningful experiences and questions.

TOUCHING YOUR WORLD (25 minutes)

This is the "take home" part of the session. Each group member will choose a weekly challenge to directly apply this session's passage in a practical way in the week ahead, as well as share prayer requests and pray for one another. Also included is a "Taking It Home" section with tips on how you can prepare for your next session.

GETTING CONNECTED

Pass your books around the room, and have group members write their names, phone numbers, e-mail addresses, and birthdays.

Name	Phone	E-mail	Birthday

FILLED WITH THE
JOY OF JESUS

PHILIPPIANS 1:1-19

In this session you'll discover ways to experience the joy we have in Jesus even in the middle of difficult circumstances.

PRE-SESSION CHECKLIST:

☐ **Leader:** Check out the Session 1 Leader Notes in the back of the book (page 76).

☐ **Food Coordinator:** If you are responsible for the Session 1 snack, see page 85.

☐ **Supplies:**

- 1 large sponge

- 1 baking pan (with at least 1-inch edges)

- 1 bucket (big enough to hold the sponge)

- Small cups for everyone in the group

- Grape juice—enough to fill everyone's cup (and more if you choose to do the **extra impact** option at the end of the session on page 17)

TASTE AND SEE (20 minutes)

While enjoying the snack, find a partner—someone you don't know very well—and take a few minutes to tell your partner a few things about yourself:

• Where did you grow up?

• What brought you to where you live now?

• What brought you to the group?

> **Tip:** If this is your first time together as a group, pass your books around to record each other's contact information (page 7), either at the start or end of this session.

Gather back together as a large group. Take turns introducing your partner to the group by sharing one thing you learned about him or her that you didn't already know. Choose one of the following questions to answer and share with the group.

• The "prison food" you had today wasn't exactly "comfort food." What *is* your favorite comfort food?

• What or who do you turn to for comfort when life becomes difficult?

 Watch the first chapter on the DVD (Philippians 1:1-19). This passage can also be found on the following pages if you would like to follow along in your book.

Philippians 1:1-19

¹This letter is from Paul and Timothy, slaves of Christ Jesus.

I am writing to all of God's holy people in Philippi who belong to Christ Jesus, including the elders and deacons.

²May God our Father and the Lord Jesus Christ give you grace and peace.

³Every time I think of you, I give thanks to my God. ⁴Whenever I pray, I make my requests for all of you with joy, ⁵for you have been my partners in spreading the Good News about Christ from the time you first heard it until now. ⁶And I am certain that God, who began the good work within you, will continue his work until it is finally finished on the day when Christ Jesus returns.

⁷So it is right that I should feel as I do about all of you, for you have a special place in my heart. You share with me the special favor of God, both in my imprisonment and in defending and confirming the truth of the Good News. ⁸God knows how much I love you and long for you with the tender compassion of Christ Jesus.

⁹I pray that your love will overflow more and more, and that you will keep on growing in knowledge and understanding. ¹⁰For I want you to understand what really matters, so that you may live pure and blameless lives until the day of Christ's return. ¹¹May you always be filled with the fruit of your salvation—the righteous character produced in your life by Jesus Christ—for this will bring much glory and praise to God.

¹²And I want you to know, my dear brothers and sisters, that everything that has happened to me here has helped to spread the Good News. ¹³For everyone here, including the whole palace guard, knows that I am in chains because of Christ. ¹⁴And because of my imprisonment, most of the believers here have gained confidence and boldly speak God's message without fear.

¹⁵It's true that some are preaching out of jealousy and rivalry. But others preach about Christ with pure motives. ¹⁶They preach because they love me, for they know I have been appointed to defend the Good News. ¹⁷Those others do not have pure motives as they preach about Christ. They preach with selfish ambition, not sincerely, intending to make my chains more painful to me. ¹⁸But that doesn't matter. Whether their motives are false or genuine, the message about Christ is being preached either way, so I rejoice. And I will continue to rejoice. ¹⁹For I know that as you pray for me and the Spirit of Jesus Christ helps me, this will lead to my deliverance.

DIGGING INTO SCRIPTURE (30 minutes)

As a group, discuss:

• What thoughts or emotions came to your mind while watching this session's Bible passage?

Tip: *To maximize participation and also have enough time to work through the session, we recommend breaking into smaller subgroups of three or four at various points during the session.*

Now break into subgroups.

Subgroup Leaders: Find a place where your subgroup can talk with few distractions. Plan to come back together in 15 minutes.

In your subgroup read Philippians 1:1-11 and the following "A Sense of History" feature, and answer the questions that follow.

A SENSE OF HISTORY
Paul and the Church at Philippi

The church at Philippi was started during Paul's second missionary journey. The first person to become a Christian there was Lydia, a businesswoman who had previously converted to Judaism (Acts 16:12-14). Lydia's entire household gave their lives to Jesus, and her home became both a place for the young church to gather and a base of operation for Paul's work.

It is widely held that at the time he wrote the epistle (letter) to the church at Philippi, Paul was in prison in Rome, under house arrest. The Philippian church showed its love for Paul by sending financial support both before and after his arrest (2 Corinthians 11:9; Philippians 4:15-16). The fact that Paul had rejected similar offers from the Corinthian church (2 Corinthians 11:7-10) suggests that his relationship with the Philippians was close enough that he could accept their generosity without compromising his ministry or feeling obligated to "pay them back."

- Think about the "prison food" you ate earlier, and then think about Paul's circumstances and his response to those circumstances in the verses you just read. If you found yourself in similar circumstances, what do you suppose your attitude would be? Why?

- According to Philippians 1:1-11, where does Paul's joy come from? How does Paul's "small group"—the church at Philippi—add to his joy?

Did you know?

Paul was also thrown into prison the first time he came to Philippi. You can learn more about this on your own this week by reading Acts 16:16-40.

- In verse 4 Paul tells us he prays for the Philippians with joy. Whom in your life do you find yourself thanking God for, and why?

Come back together as a larger group, and share any highlights or questions from your subgroup discussion.

Leader: Place the sponge on a baking pan in the middle of the group and give everyone a cup of grape juice.

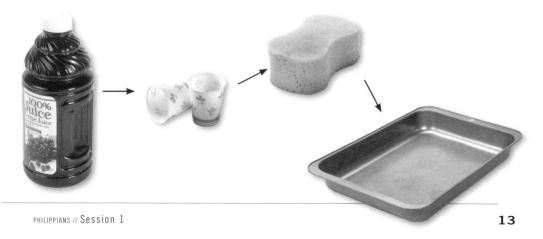

As a group, take turns pouring your cup of juice onto the sponge. Then discuss:

• Was what happened what you were expecting? Why or why not?

• How is this similar to what happens when you pour out your love for others? How is it different?

Leader: Squeeze the sponge out into the bucket, and continue the discussion.

Fast Fact: The average used kitchen sponge carries about 7.2 billion bacteria. So filling one with grape juice is the least of your worries right now.

• How are we, as individuals, like the sponge?

• When you find yourself being *squeezed* by difficult circumstances, what kind of emotions or reactions generally overflow from your life?

MAKING IT PERSONAL (15 minutes)

In your subgroups, read Philippians 1:12-19, and answer these questions:

• When was a time you were able to be joyful, despite being squeezed by your circumstances? What kept you afloat during that time?

• Practically, what do we need to fill our lives with in order to ooze joy when we find ourselves under pressure?

• Verse 12 shows us that Paul was able to put his circumstances in perspective. What challenge are you currently facing that you need a fresh perspective on so you can receive God's joy?

Come back together as a larger group, and share any highlights or questions from your subgroup discussion.

> **FYI:** It's estimated that 200 million Christians are persecuted for their faith worldwide and that an average of more than 400 Christians are killed every day for their faith in Jesus. Since Jesus' time, almost 45 million have been martyred for their faith—more than half of them since the beginning of the 20th century.

TOUCHING YOUR WORLD (25 minutes)

Review the following "weekly challenge" options, and select the challenge you'd like to do. Turn to a partner, and share your choice. Then make plans to connect with your partner sometime between now and the next session to check in and encourage one another.

☐ **HAVE AN ATTITUDE OF GRATITUDE.** Instead of letting minor problems overshadow the many blessings God has given us, commit to spend this week reflecting upon his blessings instead and to not let your circumstances distract you from that. Challenge yourself to make God's blessings the first thing you think about in the morning and the last thing you think about at night.

☐ **HELP SOMEONE WHO NEEDS IT.** Come up with a way to meet the needs of others in your group or church—either individually or in your pairs. Maybe someone you know is sick or in crisis and needs meals delivered or a home or car repair that you can help provide for financially (or maybe can even do yourself or with a group).

☐ **TURN YOUR TRIALS INTO SOMEONE ELSE'S JOY.** Maybe God has brought *you* through trials recently. Commit to find someone else at church, work, or your neighborhood going through similar trials, and encourage them regularly. (Don't do it with the idea of giving advice—simply share how God brought *you* through *your* situation. It's more important that they see that God's faithfulness is real.)

☐ **REACH OUT AS A GROUP.** Consider how your group should put its gifts and talents together to meet the needs of someone in your neighborhood or someone you know of that needs help, and then commit to do it. Give your group's Outreach Coordinator ideas on whom you would want to reach out to and how. They can then plan an event that the entire group can participate in.

Come back together as a group. Share prayer requests. Before the leader prays, take a few moments to be silent and appreciate God's goodness in your life.

Extra Impact: *Use any extra "prison food" to take the Lord's Supper together as a closing activity.*

Leader: If you haven't already, take a few minutes to review the group roles and assignments (page 82) with the group. At minimum, be sure that the food and supplies responsibilities for the next session are covered.

Until next time...

Date _____

Time _____

Place _____

Taking It Home:

1. Set a goal for how many times you'll either read through or watch on your DVD the Session 2 Bible passage (Philippians 1:20-30). Make a point to read the "A Sense of History" feature in Session 2 (page 21) prior to the next session. You may also want to review this week's passage. Let your weekly challenge partner know what goals you've set, so he or she can encourage you and help hold you accountable.

2. Touch base sometime before the next session with your weekly challenge partner to compare notes on how you're both doing with the goals you've set.

3. If you have volunteered for a role or signed up to help with food or supplies for the next session, be sure to prepare for this. The Session 2 Supplies list can be found on page 18, and the Food Coordinator instructions are on page 85.

4. **I commit to touching my world this week by showing the joy of Jesus in the following ways:**

_____

_____

_____

SESSION 2:

LIVING FULLY FOR JESUS

PHILIPPIANS 1:20-30

In this session you'll discover how to give Jesus priority in your life and how to help each other in keeping Jesus your first priority.

PRE-SESSION CHECKLIST:

☐ **Leader:** Check out the Session 2 Leader Notes in the back of the book (page 77).

☐ **Food Coordinator:** If you are responsible for the Session 2 snack, see page 85.

☐ **Supplies:**

- 1 ice cube for everyone in the group

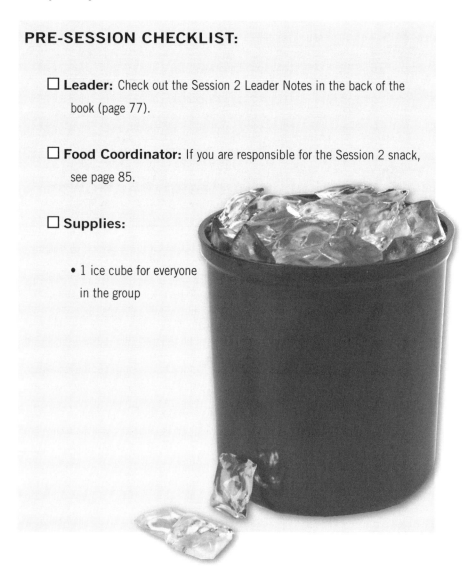

TASTE AND SEE (20 minutes)

Let's eat some pie! But first, members should each cut *one* slice of the pie and serve it to the person on their right. Take turns cutting and serving.

Once everyone has been served, go ahead and enjoy your pie! As you're eating, find a partner and share:

- What things do you have to do tomorrow?

Did you know?

Eating pie was once illegal in England. Oliver Cromwell banned it in 1644 as a pagan practice, and thus pie making and eating went "underground." The ban was lifted in 1660, not long after Cromwell was removed from power.

- What things would you *like* to get done tomorrow, if you have the time?

Gather back together as a large group, and discuss:

- If you were to illustrate your day in slices—like a pie—what would those slices look like? How fat or skinny would each slice be?

 Watch the second chapter on the DVD (Philippians 1:20-30). This passage can also be found on the following pages if you would like to follow along in your book.

Philippians 1:20-30

²⁰For I fully expect and hope that I will never be ashamed, but that I will continue to be bold for Christ, as I have been in the past. And I trust that my life will bring honor to Christ, whether I live or die. ²¹For to me, living means living for Christ, and dying is even better. ²²But if I live, I can do more fruitful work for Christ. So I really don't know which is better. ²³I'm torn between two desires: I long to go and be with Christ, which would be far better for me. ²⁴But for your sakes, it is better that I continue to live.

²⁵Knowing this, I am convinced that I will remain alive so I can continue to help all of you grow and experience the joy of your faith. ²⁶And when I come to you again, you will have even more reason to take pride in Christ Jesus because of what he is doing through me.

²⁷Above all, you must live as citizens of heaven, conducting yourselves in a manner worthy of the Good News about Christ. Then, whether I come and see you again or only hear about you, I will know that you are standing side by side, fighting together for the faith, which is the Good News.

²⁸Don't be intimidated in any way by your enemies. This will be a sign to them that they are going to be destroyed, but that you are going to be saved, even by God himself. ²⁹For you have been given not only the privilege of trusting in Christ but also the privilege of suffering for him. ³⁰We are in this struggle together. You have seen my struggle in the past, and you know that I am still in the midst of it.

A SENSE OF HISTORY

Stayin' Alive

Paul wrote this letter during the four years he was under house arrest, awaiting trial on an appeal to the Roman emperor Nero. As he was writing, Paul knew his life was on the line, yet he was convinced that this trial would not end in a death sentence (Philippians 1:25).

And he was right. It is believed that Paul lived another four to six years after writing this letter. Although it's not certain whether Paul ever visited Philippi again, we do know that after his release in A.D. 62-63, Paul resumed his travels throughout the Roman Empire—possibly as far away as Spain—spreading the Good News of Jesus' love until his rearrest and crucifixion in Rome by Nero around A.D. 67-68.

Paul lived and died in service to Christ and Christ's Kingdom, and he begged the Philippians to do the same. Paul knew they were being persecuted for their faith, just as he had been. He'd been imprisoned in Philippi when he first preached there (Acts 16:20-24), and he knew that the persecution of Christians was still a reality that the Philippian church faced daily.

DIGGING INTO SCRIPTURE (30 minutes)

As a group, discuss:

• What thoughts or emotions came to your mind while watching this session's Bible passage, whether just now or during the past week?

Now break into subgroups.

During your snack time you described what your "pie" looks like right now. Now, you're going to have the chance to *draw* it, so the rest of the group can *see* what it looks like, too.

Take a few minutes to fill in the pie in the margin of this page. Slice your pie according to the priorities in your life—some slices may be *much* bigger than other slices!

Subgroup Leaders: Be sure to keep an eye on the clock as people work on their pies. Bring people back together after two or three minutes, even if they aren't quite done yet. Take no more than 15 minutes for your discussion time.

When everyone has finished, answer the following questions:

• In one word, how did drawing your pie leave you feeling?

• When have you felt like the "slices" of your life were getting a little too thin—as if there just wasn't enough of you to go around?

Read Philippians 1:20-26 together in your subgroups, and answer the following questions:

• Based on the passage you just read, what do you think Paul's "pie chart" looked like?

• What does Paul say his reason for living is, in verse 25? How did knowing his reason for living help Paul decide what things were most important to get done?

Come back together as a larger group, and share any highlights or questions from your subgroup discussion.

Host: Bring out the ice—enough for everyone to have a cube.

Staying together as a larger group, everyone take one ice cube, put it in your right hand, and stand in a circle. Grab hands with the people on either side of you—and put the ice in between your hands. Hold hands tightly—with the ice in between—until the ice completely melts. It's going to get *really* cold, but don't let go. You're in this together!

FYI: In a field test, an average-sized ice cube took about five to seven minutes to completely melt...so stay strong; there's an end in sight!

Make the time go faster—sing a favorite song together or tell stories about the coldest you've ever been.

When all the ice has fully melted, drop hands. Blow on them, rub them together, and get your circulation back. Then read Philippians 1:27-30, and answer the following questions:

• What was it like as you held onto the ice—and it got colder? Did it make it better or worse knowing that your partners were going through the same thing? Explain.

• How does standing together as a group when we're struggling help each of us keep Jesus a priority in our lives?

MAKING IT PERSONAL (15 minutes)

Reread Philippians 1:20-26, and answer these questions:

• How would you describe your own reason for living at this time in your life?

• How would your life look differently if you changed your priorities to living fully for Jesus?

• What do you need to do to give Jesus the priority he deserves in your life? How can you help each other keep Jesus as your first priority?

TOUCHING YOUR WORLD (25 minutes)

Review the following weekly challenge options, and then select the challenge you'd like to do. Turn to a partner, and share your choice. Then make plans to connect with your partner sometime between now and the next session to check in and encourage one another.

☐ **PRIORITIZE.** On your own time, create another pie chart—this time, for the *week* ahead. Identify the slices of your life that you'd like to be the biggest. Look at that chart in the morning each day, and work hard to live out those priorities—spend more time with your family, talk to God more often, don't procrastinate at work or school. Do whatever it takes to make your priorities the biggest slices in your life.

☐ **STAND TOGETHER.** Think of someone in your life who is really struggling right now—in faith, in finances, in health, in anything—and commit to contact that person each day this week. Call the person, get together for coffee, send him or her a card. Come up with unique ideas for supporting that person each day. In doing so, you are standing side by side as the person fights his or her battles.

☐ **FIGHT TOGETHER.** As a group, commit to fight for Jesus…together. Come up with an idea that works well for everyone in your group. If everyone has a passion to end homelessness, you could volunteer at a local shelter together; if your group is made up of artists, you could hold a free community art show or poetry reading and ask your members to create a piece of work that represents the love of Jesus to others. Come up with an idea that fits your group, and do it!

Come back together as a group. Share prayer requests, and then pray for everyone's needs. Express your confidence in Jesus to meet every one of your group members' needs.

Until next time...

Date _____

Time _____

Place _____

Taking It Home:

1. Set a goal for how many times you'll either read through or watch on your DVD the Session 3 Bible passage (Philippians 2:1-18). Make a point to read the "A Sense of History" feature in Session 3 (page 32) before the next session. You may also want to review this week's passage—or even watch the entire book of Philippians straight through. (It takes about 16 minutes.) Let your weekly challenge partner know what goals you've set, so he or she can encourage you and help hold you accountable.

2. Touch base sometime before the next session with your weekly challenge partner to compare notes on how you're both doing with the goals you've set.

3. If you have volunteered for a role or signed up to help with food or supplies for the next session, be sure to prepare for this. The Session 3 supplies list can be found on page 28, and the Food Coordinator instructions are on page 85.

4. **I commit to touching my world this week by living fully for Jesus in the following ways:**

_____

_____

_____

_____

SESSION 3:

SHOWING TRUE HUMILITY

PHILIPPIANS 2:1-18

In this session you'll learn about the amazing love and humility of Jesus and how we can show Jesus' kind of humility to others.

PRE-SESSION CHECKLIST:

☐ **Leader:** Check out the Session 3 Leader Notes in the back of the book (page 78).

☐ **Food Coordinator:** If you are responsible for the Session 3 snack, see page 85.

☐ **Supplies:**

- 1 glass bowl or food storage container for each subgroup

- Enough rocks to fill the above containers

- 1 pitcher of water for each subgroup

- 1 bath towel for each subgroup

- 1 medium or large candle

- Matches

TASTE AND SEE (20 minutes)

Today's session starts with a snack served in two courses. As you eat your first course, turn to a partner and share:

• What's the fanciest meal you've ever had?

• How did it feel to be served such elegant food?

Gather back together as a large group.

Food Coordinator: Serve the second course to the group now.

After you've "enjoyed" your second course, answer the following questions:

• Which course did you like better? Why?

• How would you describe the two courses? What might they symbolize?

 Watch the third chapter on the DVD (Philippians 2:1-18). This passage can also be found on the following pages.

Philippians 2:1-18

[1]Is there any encouragement from belonging to Christ? Any comfort from his love? Any fellowship together in the Spirit? Are your hearts tender and compassionate? [2]Then make me truly happy by agreeing wholeheartedly with each other, loving one another, and working together with one mind and purpose.

[3]Don't be selfish; don't try to impress others. Be humble, thinking of others as better than yourselves. [4]Don't look out only for your own interests, but take an interest in others, too.

[5]You must have the same attitude that Christ Jesus had.

[6]Though he was God,
he did not think of equality with God as something to cling to.
[7]Instead, he gave up his divine privileges; he took the humble position of a slave and was born as a human being.
When he appeared in human form,
[8]he humbled himself in obedience to God and died a criminal's death on a cross.

[9]Therefore, God elevated him to the place of highest honor
and gave him the name above all other names,
[10]that at the name of Jesus every knee should bow,
in heaven and on earth and under the earth,
[11]and every tongue confess that Jesus Christ is Lord,
to the glory of God the Father.

[12]Dear friends, you always followed my instructions when I was with you. And now that I am away, it is even more important. Work hard to show the results of your salvation, obeying God with deep reverence and fear. [13]For God is working in you, giving you the desire and the power to do what pleases him.

[14]Do everything without complaining and arguing, [15]so that no one can criticize you. Live clean, innocent lives as children of God, shining like bright lights in a world full of crooked and perverse people. [16]Hold firmly to the word of life; then, on the day of Christ's return, I will be proud that I did not run the race in vain and that my work was not useless. [17]But I will rejoice even if I lose my life, pouring it out like a liquid offering to God, just like your faithful service is an offering to God. And I want all of you to share that joy. [18]Yes, you should rejoice, and I will share your joy.

A SENSE OF HISTORY

A Hymn to Humility

Verses 5-11 of this chapter are the centerpiece of Paul's letter to the Philippians. In driving home his point, Paul draws from what is believed to be a New Testament "hymn" that most first-century Christians likely knew by heart.

In one of the earliest historical descriptions of the Christian church, the Roman author Pliny wrote (around A.D. 112) that followers of Jesus "were in the habit of meeting...before it was light, when they sang an anthem to Christ as God, and bound themselves by a solemn oath not to commit any wicked deed."

The earliest known hymn outside of the Bible (referenced by St. Justin around 150) gives a sense of what early church worship must have looked and felt like:

O gladsome light
Of the Father Immortal,
And of the celestial
Sacred and blessed
Jesus, our Savior!

Now to the sunset
Again hast thou brought us;
And seeing the evening
Twilight, we bless thee,
Praise thee, adore thee!

Father omnipotent!
Son, the Life-giver!
Spirit, the Comforter!
Worthy at all times
Of worship and wonder!

In Ephesians 5:19 and again in Colossians 3:16, Paul encourages the churches to sing "psalms and hymns and spiritual songs," and in the hymn of Philippians 2:5-11, Paul highlights Jesus as the supreme model for humility and service. As we consider the Incarnation—the awesome Son of God taking on human flesh, living in lowly circumstances, and then dying a criminal's death—we can only stand amazed at this picture of *true humility*.

DIGGING INTO SCRIPTURE (30 minutes)

As a group, discuss:

• What thoughts or emotions came to your mind while watching this session's Bible passage, whether just now or during the past week?

Read Philippians 2:1-4 together, and answer the following questions:

• How do you think most people would define *humility*?

• Do you believe what Paul is saying in verses 2-4 is *really* possible? Why or why not?

At this time, break up into subgroups.

Subgroup Leaders: Find a place where your subgroup can talk with few distractions. Plan to come back together in 15 minutes.

From the supplies that are set out on the table, each subgroup should take a container, rocks, a water pitcher, and a bath towel.

Together, fill your container with as many rocks as you want. As you add rocks, imagine that your rocks represent "self"—personal ambitions, goals, desires, dreams, choices, control...*stuff.*

> ***Did you know?*** *Ever wonder what "humble pie" really is? It has little to do with true humility! Humble pie was made from the organs of a deer—the "humbles." It was eaten by servants and other members of the lower class who could not afford meat; thus, "eating humble pie" implied that someone was being lowered or humiliated.*

Subgroup Leader: Pour water into your container, leaving a little extra space at the top.

As a subgroup, answer the following:

• Think about the rocks you put in your container. How does your own definition of humility compare or contrast with the ideas symbolized by those rocks?

Definition: Webster's New World College Dictionary *defines the word* humble *this way:* "having or showing a consciousness of one's defects or shortcomings; not proud; not self-assertive; modest."

• See the note in the margin, and compare the dictionary definition of *humble* with Philippians 2:5-11. What's similar? What's different?

Remove the rocks from your container, and place them on a towel. Look at the water level now; answer the following:

• Jesus promised us "*living* water" (John 4:10; 7:37-39). How do the "rocks" in our lives keep us from receiving Jesus' life? from sharing it with others?

Fast Fact: The world's biggest rock, known as Mt. Augustus (also called "Burringurrah" by the local Aboriginal people) is in Australia. It is 858 meters tall and covers 4800 hectares. (Not up to speed on metric conversion? Translation: It's more than half a mile tall and more than 18 square miles in area.)

Subgroup Leader: Fill your container one more time—with just water.

Think of this as being filled with God's presence and directed wholly by his will. Now, everyone pick up a rock, and while you're holding it, answer the following:

• When have you been so filled up with your own concerns, worries, ideas, or goals that you weren't truly "filled" with Jesus? How did it prevent you from being truly humble?

Now, put your rocks down, and answer:

• Share an example from your own life of how you were able to move from conflict to unity with another Christian. How did you do it? How did your experience change the way you approach differences with other Christians?

> *"Humility is not my forte, and whenever I dwell for any length of time on my own shortcomings, they gradually begin to seem mild, harmless, rather engaging little things, not at all like the staring defects in other people's characters."*
>
> *—Margaret Halsey*
>
> *Ever felt this way?*
> *Be honest!*

Come back together as a larger group and share any highlights or questions from your subgroup discussion.

MAKING IT PERSONAL (15 minutes)

Leader: Dim the lights, place a candle in the center of the room, and light it. Have a volunteer read Philippians 2:12-18 aloud, while everyone else focuses on the words being read.

Following the reading, discuss the following questions:

• Which words or phrases jumped out at you as descriptions of true humility? Why?

• In John 8:12, Jesus says, "I am the light of the world." In Philippians 2:15, Paul says that by being filled with Jesus' presence, *you* can shine like "bright lights" in a dark world. How does having Jesus' kind of humility change your relationships with others—Christian or non-Christian?

> **Check it out!**
> One great example of humility is John the Baptist's response to Jesus: "He must become greater and greater, and I must become less and less" (John 3:30). How can you live this out?

• Think of a relationship in which it's been tough to live out the unity described in Philippians 2:2. How could you show Christ-like humility in that relationship?

TOUCHING YOUR WORLD (25 minutes)

Review the following weekly challenge options, and then select the challenge you'd like to do. Turn to a partner, and share your choice. Then make plans to connect with your partner sometime between now and the next session to check in and encourage one another.

☐ **REMOVE THE "ROCKS" IN YOUR LIFE.** Think about the struggles with "self" you face: self-centeredness, pride, a need to impress others, a critical attitude toward others. Ask God to reveal one area you need to focus on, and then identify one way you can address this struggle in your life right now.

☐ **TAKE ON A "HUMBLE" TASK.** Follow Jesus' example by choosing a thankless, undesirable act of service you can commit to do for someone else this week, such as scrubbing toilets (at home or at church), picking up trash in your neighborhood park, scrubbing a friend's floors, or baby-sitting a neighbor's children. As you take this on, remind yourself of Jesus' amazing example of humility.

☐ **MINISTER AS A GROUP.** Plan a service opportunity in which your group can be like Christ through showing love and kindness to people living in meager circumstances. Your group could serve a meal at a soup kitchen or volunteer to work as a cleaning crew at a homeless shelter. At the end of your service time, talk as a group about what God taught you during the experience. How did God enlarge your understanding of humility? What did he teach you about his love?

Come back together as a group. Share prayer requests, and then pray for everyone's needs. Pray that each person in the group would be able show Christ's humility in each situation he or she faces.

Until next time...

Date _____

Time _____

Place _____

Taking It Home:

1. Set a goal for how many times you'll either read through or watch on your DVD the Session 4 Bible passage (Philippians 2:19-30). Make a point to read the "A Sense of History" feature in Session 4 (page 43) before the next session. You may also want to review this week's passage—or even watch the entire book of Philippians straight through. (It takes about 16 minutes.) Let your weekly challenge partner know what goals you've set, so he or she can encourage you and help hold you accountable.

2. Touch base sometime before the next session with your weekly challenge partner to compare notes on how you're both doing with the goals you've set.

3. If you have volunteered for a role or signed up to help with food or supplies for the next session, be sure to prepare for this. The Session 4 supplies list can be found on page 40, and the Food Coordinator instructions are on page 86.

4. **I commit to touching my world this week by showing humility toward others in the following ways:**

_____

_____

_____

_____

_____

_____

_____

SESSION 4:

HONORING THOSE WHO SERVE US

PHILIPPIANS 2:19-30

In this session you'll explore practical ways to honor those who serve us.

PRE-SESSION CHECKLIST:

☐ **Leader:** Check out the Session 4 Leader Notes in the back of the book (page 79).

☐ **Food Coordinator:** If you are responsible for the Session 4 snack, see page 86.

☐ **Supplies:**

- One 3x5-inch index card for everyone in the group (optional)

- 1 pen or pencil for everyone in the group (optional)

TASTE AND SEE (20 minutes)

Tonight's snack is a very special one—it's an old family recipe. Enjoy! While you're enjoying your snack, turn to a partner and discuss the following:

• What's a traditional dish or recipe that's served in your own family?

• What's one memory you associate with that dish?

> **Extra Impact:** *You may have your own family recipe you'd like to share with the group. If so, write it up on an index card. If someone is willing to volunteer to compile these recipes for the group so everyone can enjoy them, pass your card on to him or her.*

Gather back together as a large group.

Food Coordinator: Pass out the recipe cards for tonight's snack.

Answer the following question:

• This snack's "reputation" preceded it. How did knowing this snack was a "family favorite" affect your experience while eating it?

 Watch the fourth chapter on the DVD (Philippians 2:19-30).

Philippians 2:19-30

[19]If the Lord Jesus is willing, I hope to send Timothy to you soon for a visit. Then he can cheer me up by telling me how you are getting along. [20]I have no one else like Timothy, who genuinely cares about your welfare. [21]All the others care only for themselves and not for what matters to Jesus Christ. [22]But you know how Timothy has proved himself. Like a son with his father, he has served with me in preaching the Good News. [23]I hope to send him to you just as soon as I find out what is going to happen to me here. [24]And I have confidence from the Lord that I myself will come to see you soon.

[25]Meanwhile, I thought I should send Epaphroditus back to you. He is a true brother, co-worker, and fellow soldier. And he was your messenger to help me in my need. [26]I am sending him because he has been longing to see you, and he was very distressed that you heard he was ill. [27]And he certainly was ill; in fact, he almost died. But God had mercy on him—and also on me, so that I would not have one sorrow after another.

[28]So I am all the more anxious to send him back to you, for I know you will be glad to see him, and then I will not be so worried about you. [29]Welcome him with Christian love and with great joy, and give him the honor that people like him deserve. [30]For he risked his life for the work of Christ, and he was at the point of death while doing for me what you couldn't do from far away.

A SENSE OF HISTORY

A Couple Good Men

In some ways, this particular passage seems out of place. Paul is telling the Philippians to shine brightly for Christ, then suddenly he is conveying his intent to send Timothy and Epaphroditus to them, and then just as quickly he returns to encouraging the Philippians to rejoice in the Lord. Why does Paul take this "detour"?

Perhaps it was because his description of someone who has the attitude of Christ (Philippians 2:1-11) and who shines brightly for Christ (Philippians 2:12-18) reminded him of Timothy and Epaphroditus. Even as Paul wrote, "You must have the same attitude that Christ Jesus had," perhaps Timothy and Epaphroditus came to mind as living examples of this attitude.

We know nothing about Epaphroditus aside from what we read in this passage, although later in this letter (Philippians 4:18) Paul specifically states that Epaphroditus came with gifts the Philippian church had sent along with him.

We know considerably more about Timothy. We first hear about him in Acts 16. He met Paul during Paul's second trip to Lystra, a town in Asia Minor (now Turkey). As Paul had been stoned and left for dead the *first* time he visited Lystra (Acts 14:8-20), Timothy knew what the cost of following Jesus could be. Nonetheless Timothy accompanied Paul, helping him plant churches in Corinth, Thessalonica, Philippi, and Ephesus. Later, he became the first bishop of the Ephesian church. Tradition teaches that Timothy did pay the ultimate cost for serving Jesus, being martyred in Ephesus for protesting the festivals in honor of the goddess Artemis (Diana) around A.D. 97.

DIGGING INTO SCRIPTURE (30 minutes)

As a group, discuss:

• What thoughts or emotions came to your mind while watching this session's Bible passage?

Now break into subgroups.

Subgroup Leaders: Plan to come back together in 20 minutes.

Describe a person that you know well—but who no one else in your subgroup knows. After everyone's had a chance to describe someone, answer the following questions:

• What sounded appealing about each person described?

• When has someone been recommended to you (or recommended by you to someone else), and that person then proved himself or herself—or failed to? How did that affect how you approached future "recommendations"?

Read Philippians 2:19-24 together in your subgroup, and answer the following questions:

• Imagine being a Philippian reading this for the first time. What impressions would you have had of Timothy?

• In verse 22, Paul takes pride in being a "father" to Timothy. Who has been a "father" or "mother" to you—someone whose example you have followed in your faith? How has your association with that person helped you?

• How have you been a servant to others—maybe even a "father" or "mother" to another Christian? How has that changed your own life?

Come back together as a larger group, and share any highlights or questions from your subgroup discussion.

> **On your own time:**
> Read Paul's "fatherly" advice to Timothy in 1 Timothy 4:6-16.

MAKING IT PERSONAL (15 minutes)

Break back into your subgroups.

Choose one person in your subgroup to be a "messenger." Everyone else should assign the messenger a message to give to a member of another subgroup. The message could be several words, an action such as a hug, or even a written note.

Once each messenger has delivered his or her message, switch roles. Continue until each member has "dispatched" a message, and then come back together as a larger group and discuss:

• How comfortable were you sending your message through another person?

• How comfortable were you delivering the message?

Reread Philippians 2:19-30, and answer the following:

• Take a few moments to think about the people who have served you or brought a message of hope to you. Who's a "Timothy" in your life right now—one who leads by serving? Who's an "Epaphroditus"—one who serves behind the scenes?

• As a group, brainstorm a list of ways you could honor those people you've just named. What things can you begin putting into practice, and how will you do it?

TOUCHING YOUR WORLD (25 minutes)

Review the following weekly challenge options, and select the challenge you'd like to do. Turn to a partner, and share your choice. Then make plans to connect with your partner sometime between now and the next session to check in and encourage one another.

☐ **RECOMMEND YOUR FRIENDS—ALL OF THEM.** Make a conscious effort to speak highly of your friends this week. Praise them—to their faces and to others. Friends are a gift from God, so be excited about them this week, and share your excitement! And not just your human friends, either—speak highly of your greatest friend: Jesus.

☐ **BECOME A MENTOR.** Maybe God has helped you through tough times or grown you as you've served God faithfully. Others need to hear your story and benefit from your experience and example. Is there someone in your life whom you could encourage and support regularly? If so, commit to call that person this week and set up a time to get together. They'll be honored that you thought of them.

☐ **SERVE A SERVANT.** Does your church support missionaries? How about someone who shares Jesus' love with troubled teens? someone who's working with the Red Cross? Send them a card and a care package; pray for them; e-mail them; call and ask how they're doing. Don't restrict your service to Christian servants, either—if there are local public servants you can honor as well (whether it's your mayor, your mail carrier, or the person who bags your groceries), identify a way to honor them, and then do it.

Come back together as a group. Share prayer requests, and then pray for everyone's needs. Be sure to thank God for each person in your group and what they bring to it each week, even if they don't have a prayer request this week.

Until next time...

Date _____

Time _____

Place _____

Taking It Home:

1. Set a goal for how many times you'll either read through or watch on your DVD the Session 5 Bible passage (Philippians 3:1-21). Make a point to read the "A Sense of History" feature in Session 5 (page 54) before the next session. Let your weekly challenge partner know what goals you've set, so he or she can encourage you and help hold you accountable.

2. Touch base sometime before the next session with your weekly challenge partner to compare notes on how you're both doing with the goals you've set.

3. If you have volunteered for a role or signed up to help with food or supplies for the next session, be sure to prepare for this. The Session 5 supplies list can be found on page 50, and the Food Coordinator instructions are on page 86.

4. **I commit to touching my world this week by honoring those around me in the following ways:**

_____

_____

_____

_____

_____

_____

SESSION5:

CHOOSING TO LOOK LIKE JESUS

PHILIPPIANS 3:1-21

In this session you'll discover how we can choose to pattern our lives after Jesus.

PRE-SESSION CHECKLIST:

☐ **Leader:** Check out the Session 5 Leader Notes in the back of the book (page 80).

☐ **Food Coordinator:** If you are responsible for the Session 5 snack, see page 86.

☐ **Supplies:**

• Paper—at least two sheets per group member

• 1 pen or pencil for everyone in the group

TASTE AND SEE (20 minutes)

Food Coordinator: Serve up the "orders" you took from the group.

Enjoy your dessert, and eat *only* that dessert—no sharing. Look around and see what other group members are eating, and notice what their expressions are as they enjoy *their* desserts.

As you eat, discuss the following questions:

• What's special about your choice of dessert?

• Which desserts, if any, make you wonder if you should have made a different choice? Why?

• What's a decision you've reconsidered recently? What gave you second thoughts about it?

 Watch the fifth chapter on the DVD (Philippians 3:1-21).

Philippians 3:1-21

[1]Whatever happens, my dear brothers and sisters, rejoice in the Lord. I never get tired of telling you these things, and I do it to safeguard your faith.

[2]Watch out for those dogs, those people who do evil, those mutilators who say you must be circumcised to be saved. [3]For we who worship by the Spirit of God are the ones who are truly circumcised. We rely on what Christ Jesus has done for us. We put no confidence in human effort, [4]though I could have confidence in my own effort if anyone could. Indeed, if others have reason for confidence in their own efforts, I have even more!

[5]I was circumcised when I was eight days old. I am a pure-blooded citizen of Israel and a member of the tribe of Benjamin—a real Hebrew if there ever was one! I was a member of the Pharisees, who demand the strictest obedience to the Jewish law. [6]I was so zealous that I harshly persecuted the church. And as for righteousness, I obeyed the law without fault.

[7]I once thought these things were valuable, but now I consider them worthless because of what Christ has done. [8]Yes, everything else is worthless when compared with the infinite value of knowing Christ Jesus my Lord. For his sake I have discarded everything else, counting it all as garbage, so that I could gain Christ [9]and become one with him. I no longer count on my own righteousness through obeying the law; rather, I become righteous through faith in Christ. For God's way of making us right with himself depends on faith. [10]I want to know Christ and experience the mighty power that raised him from the dead. I want to suffer with him, sharing in his death, [11]so that one way or another I will experience the resurrection from the dead!

¹²I don't mean to say that I have already achieved these things or that I have already reached perfection. But I press on to possess that perfection for which Christ Jesus first possessed me. ¹³No, dear brothers and sisters, I have not achieved it, but I focus on this one thing: Forgetting the past and looking forward to what lies ahead, ¹⁴I press on to reach the end of the race and receive the heavenly prize for which God, through Christ Jesus, is calling us.

¹⁵Let all who are spiritually mature agree on these things. If you disagree on some point, I believe God will make it plain to you. ¹⁶But we must hold on to the progress we have already made.

¹⁷Dear brothers and sisters, pattern your lives after mine, and learn from those who follow our example. ¹⁸For I have told you often before, and I say it again with tears in my eyes, that there are many whose conduct shows they are really enemies of the cross of Christ. ¹⁹They are headed for destruction. Their god is their appetite, they brag about shameful things, and they think only about this life here on earth. ²⁰But we are citizens of heaven, where the Lord Jesus Christ lives. And we are eagerly waiting for him to return as our Savior. ²¹He will take our weak mortal bodies of ours and change them into glorious bodies like his own, using the same power with which he will bring everything under his control.

A SENSE OF HISTORY

Running the Race in Paul's Time

Races in Paul's time were popularized by the Greeks—Paul might have even been acquainted with the Isthmian games at Corinth. In those days, the prize for winning a race was placed at the end of the race, so runners could keep their eyes on it as they ran. Therefore, those who could avoid distractions and focus on the prize had the best chance of winning. In many of the games at this time, the prize was a simple laurel wreath placed on the head. This is where the phrase "resting on your laurels" comes from. Paul tells the Philippians much of the same thing in this passage: "Forgetting the past and looking forward to what lies ahead, I press on to reach the end of the race" (Philippians 3:13b-14a).

Except Paul's prize wasn't a laurel wreath—it was to become like Christ. Paul ran the race to win that prize, avoiding all distractions—

whether it was something from the present or a tradition from the past. Paul was so focused on serving Christ and becoming more like him that everything else faded into second place. This was the focus that made him a winner.

DIGGING INTO SCRIPTURE (30 minutes)

As a group, discuss:

• What thoughts or emotions came to your mind while watching this session's Bible passage?

Host: Be sure everyone has a sheet of paper and something to write with.

As a group, listen to someone with a strong reading voice read Philippians 3:1-21. As you listen, write down the words or phrases that strike you "at a gut level."

Now break into subgroups.

Subgroup Leaders: Take no more than 15 minutes for your discussion time.

Answer the following questions:

• Which words and phrases did you write down? What made you react to those particular words and phrases?

• What does Paul mean in verses 7-8 when he calls his past accomplishments "worthless" in comparison to knowing Jesus? Is he putting himself down? Why or why not?

> ***On your own time:***
> *This is not the only time that Paul used the image of running a race to get his point across. Read also what he says in 1 Corinthians 9:24-27 and 2 Timothy 4:7-8. Perhaps he was even a fan of the sport!*

- If you had to pick one area of your life where could you honestly instruct others to "pattern your lives after mine" (verse 17), what would it be? (No false humility here—be thankful for what Jesus has done in this area of your life.)

Come back together as a larger group, and share any highlights or questions from your subgroup discussion.

Now you're going to learn a little art forgery. Really!

Host: Give everyone another sheet of paper, and make sure everyone has a writing surface (like a tabletop or book).

Break into pairs. In your pair, whoever's birthday comes earlier in the year will be the "artist," and the other will be the "forger."

Artists: Draw any kind of picture you want, taking no more than two minutes. Don't show your picture to your partner. When you're done, help your partner forge the picture you just drew. *One catch:* You cannot let the forger see the original "work of art." He or she will need to listen as you tell him or her what to draw— and try to duplicate it *based on the description you're giving.*

Fast Fact: Before there was a commercial art market, copying a master was a tribute, not a forgery. In past centuries, apprentices studied painting techniques by working under a master, copying the master's works and style.

Take no more than five minutes to do this. When everyone is finished, come back together as a larger group, and see how close your forgers got to the original!

Then answer the following questions:

• **Forgers:** How close did you come to reproducing the original "work of art"? What descriptions helped you visualize what needed to be drawn?

• How would it have been easier if you could actually have *seen* what the artists drew?

• **Everyone:** How is patterning your lives after Jesus like your forger's attempts to reproduce someone else's "work of art"? How is it unlike it?

• Why is it important to see Christ-likeness modeled? How is seeing it different from hearing it described?

• Who are *your* models (name one or two)? What's one thing you've learned about following Jesus from them?

MAKING IT PERSONAL (15 minutes)

As a larger group, read Philippians 3:12-14 again, and answer the following questions:

- At this moment, where are you in the race Paul describes here? Are you a front-runner? middle of the pack? lagging behind? hobbling? barely out of the gate?

- If becoming more like Jesus is really your goal in life, how does dwelling on the past affect your ability to "reach the end of the race and receive the heavenly prize" (verse 14)?

- If you imitated Paul's choice by "forgetting the past and looking forward to what lies ahead" (verse 13), what would be the most important thing for you to put behind you? How would you describe "what lies ahead" for you?

TOUCHING YOUR WORLD (25 minutes)

Review the following weekly challenge options, and then select the challenge you'd like to do. Turn to a partner, and share your choice. Then make plans to connect with your partner sometime between now and the next session to check in and encourage one another.

☐ **GIVE YOURSELF AN "AUDIT."** Look through recent bank statements to see where your money is going. Sit down with your day timer or calendar and do the same thing. What are you spending time and money on? Work? Family? Television, surfing the Internet, or playing computer games? What does it say about the choices you're making in life? Take time to think about how you can improve those choices.

☐ **BURY YOUR PAST—LITERALLY.** Have you been bound by past pain and trauma? Maybe past mistakes or things that happened in your childhood? Or perhaps your problem is that you have idealized the past or have been resting on your past "laurels." Determine to let these things die. Write them all down, pray to God to give you the ability to let those things go, and then bury the paper(s) in the ground. Thank God for your past—because it has made you who you are today—but let it die so that your future can live.

☐ **SET A GOAL FOR YOUR GROUP.** What "lies ahead" for your group? Will you end after next week's final session, or will you move on to something more? A group which just tries to "tread water" generally dies. Set a group growth goal. Discuss ways you can reach out and include new people. If you choose this option, plan to work on it next week as well.

Come back together as a group. Share prayer requests, and then pray for everyone's needs. Focus on the choices each person has made tonight to look more like Jesus.

Until next time...

Date _____

Time _____

Place _____

Taking It Home:

1. Set a goal for how many times you'll either read through or watch on your DVD the Session 6 Bible passage (Philippians 4:1-23). Make a point to read the "A Sense of History" feature in Session 6 (page 66) before the next session. If you haven't yet, now would be a good time to watch the entire book of Philippians in one sitting. (It takes about 16 minutes to watch the entire book.) Let your weekly challenge partner know what goals you've set, so he or she can encourage you and help hold you accountable.

2. Touch base sometime before the next session with your weekly challenge partner to compare notes on how you're both doing with the goals you've set.

3. If you have volunteered for a role or signed up to help with food for the next session, be sure to prepare for this. The Food Coordinator instructions are on page 86.

4. I commit to touching my world this week by releasing my past and choosing to look like Jesus in the present in the following ways:

_____

_____

_____

_____

_____

_____

_____

SESSION 6:

EVERYTHING WE NEED IN JESUS

PHILIPPIANS 4:1-23

In this session you'll reflect on what it means to have the peace and joy we can only find in Jesus.

PRE-SESSION CHECKLIST:

☐ **Leader:** Check out the Session 6 Leader Notes in the back of the book (page 81).

☐ **Food Coordinator:** If you are responsible for the Session 6 snack, see page 86.

☐ **Supplies:**
None

TASTE AND SEE (20 minutes)

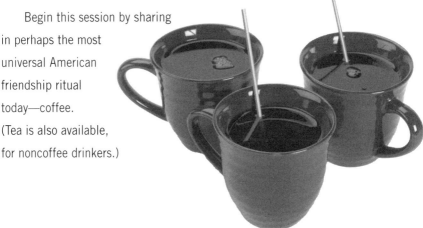

Begin this session by sharing in perhaps the most universal American friendship ritual today—coffee. (Tea is also available, for noncoffee drinkers.)

While you're enjoying your beverage, discuss the following questions:

• Why is drinking coffee or tea together such a popular modern ritual?

• How does the ritual of a "coffee break" bring peace to your day? How long does that "peace" usually last?

• What other things do we use to try to bring peace to our lives?

 Watch the final chapter on the DVD (Philippians 4:1-23).

Philippians 4:1-23

[1]Therefore, my dear brothers and sisters, stay true to the Lord. I love you and long to see you, dear friends, for you are my joy and the crown I receive for my work.

[2]Now I appeal to Euodia and Syntyche. Please, because you belong to the Lord, settle your disagreement. [3]And I ask you, my true partner, to help these two women, for they worked hard with me in telling others the Good News. They worked along with Clement and the rest of my co-workers, whose names are written in the Book of Life.

[4]Always be full of joy in the Lord. I say it again—rejoice! [5]Let everyone see that you are considerate in all you do. Remember, the Lord is coming soon.

[6]Don't worry about anything; instead, pray about everything. Tell God what you need, and thank him for all he has done. [7]Then you will experience God's peace, which exceeds anything we can understand. His peace will guard your hearts and minds as you live in Christ Jesus.

[8]And now, dear brothers and sisters, one final thing. Fix your thoughts on what is true, and honorable, and right, and pure, and lovely, and admirable. Think about things that are excellent and worthy of praise. [9]Keep putting into practice all you learned and received from me—everything you heard from me and saw me doing. Then the God of peace will be with you.

[10]How I praise the Lord that you are concerned about me again. I know you have always been concerned for me, but you didn't have the chance to help me. [11]Not that I was ever in need, for I have learned how to be content with whatever I have.

[12]I know how to live on almost nothing or with everything. I have learned the secret of living in every situation, whether it is with a full stomach or empty, with plenty or little. [13]For I can do everything through Christ, who gives me strength. [14]Even so, you have done well to share with me in my present difficulty.

[15]As you know, you Philippians were the only ones who gave me financial help when I first brought you the Good News and then traveled on from Macedonia. No other church did this. [16]Even when I was in Thessalonica you sent help more than once. [17]I don't say this because I want a gift from you. Rather, I want you to receive a reward for your kindness.

[18]At the moment I have all I need—and more! I am generously supplied with the gifts you sent me with Epaphroditus. They are a sweet-smelling sacrifice that is acceptable to and pleasing to God. [19]And this same God who takes care of me will supply all your needs from his glorious riches, which have been given to us in Christ Jesus.

[20]Now glory be to God our Father forever and ever! Amen.

[21]Give my greetings to each of God's holy people—all who belong to Christ Jesus. The brothers who are with me send you their greetings. [22]And all the rest of God's people send you greetings, too, especially those in Caesar's household.

[23]May the grace of the Lord Jesus Christ be with your spirit.

A SENSE OF HISTORY

The Bare Necessities

What we think of as "the bare necessities" is far different from what people thought of in Paul's day. Of course, people of those times didn't have things like televisions, laptop computers, or iPods. But their homes were even simpler than we often imagine.

Windows in that time were just holes in the wall without glass or often any kind of covering at all. Light came from simple oil lamps, which often were the bases of broken jars, filled with olive oil and a wick of flax or wool. Tables were low to the ground and chairs were a luxury. A bed was most often a straw mat, although "better-off" people might have a couch with legs.

Most people had no more than a couple of changes of clothing, and some only had one. Jewish law required that garments taken in pledge from a poor person be returned by sunset because it may have been their only garment, and they would have needed it for warmth (Deuteronomy 24:12-13).

When Paul wrote, "I have all I need," he was under house arrest—and therefore faced what most of us would consider serious hardship. Considering this and the other circumstances he had already faced before his imprisonment, Paul's statement becomes all the more significant.

DIGGING INTO SCRIPTURE (30 minutes)

As a group, discuss:

• What thoughts or emotions came to your mind while watching this session's Bible passage?

• What have your overall impressions been as you've interacted with the book of Philippians? How has God spoken to you through this study?

Now break into subgroups.

Subgroup Leaders: Plan to come back together in 10 minutes.

Read Philippians 4:1-13, and answer the following questions:

• From what you sense of Paul's mood here, is he closer to being on an emotional mountaintop or in a valley? What lifts him up, and what brings him down?

• When have you, like Paul, found strength and peace in difficult circumstances? In what ways did God provide what you needed during this time?

Come back together as a larger group, and share any highlights or questions from your subgroup discussion.

Break back into subgroups—make sure there are at *least* four people in each subgroup this time. (If there aren't at least eight people in your group, do the following as a larger group instead.)

Have a volunteer stand up and shut his or her eyes, crossing his or her arms over his or her chest. The other members of your group or subgroup should stand in a tight circle about 3 feet behind this person.

When everyone's in position, ask the person to fall backward, keeping his or her legs and body straight, while the other group members catch him or her.

Take turns in your groups or subgroups doing this. (Use wisdom here, though—anyone in danger of not being caught due to height or weight or who is otherwise unable to do this physical activity is free to "take a pass.")

Read Philippians 4:14-23, and answer the following:

• When you let yourself fall—or were about to catch someone—were you anxious or at peace and confident? Why?

• How do you think the Philippian church did at "catching" Paul? What things did they do to hold him up?

• How does knowing that others are there to catch you help you to have God's peace?

• What can you do to let others know that you'll be there to catch them if they fall?

If you did this activity in subgroups, come back together as a larger group, and share any highlights or questions from your discussion.

MAKING IT PERSONAL (15 minutes)

Reread Philippians 4:4-12, and answer the following questions:

• How can doing the things Paul suggests in verses 4-9 give you God's peace? Give personal examples if possible.

• Which things in this passage do you have a hard time "putting into practice"?

• When it comes to practicing the "secret" of being "content with whatever I have," how would you rate yourself on a scale of one (it is the winter of my discontent) to 10 (move over, Paul)? Explain.

• What's one change you've been challenged to make in this study that will help you to better know the peace and joy of Jesus?

> **"**When life on earth is ending, people don't surround themselves with objects. What we want around us is people—people we love and have relationships with. In our final moments we all realize that relationships are what life is all about. Wisdom is learning that truth sooner rather than later.**"**
>
> —*Rick Warren,*
> The Purpose-Driven Life

TOUCHING YOUR WORLD (25 minutes)

Review the following weekly challenge options, and then select the challenge you'd like to do. Turn to a partner, and share your choice. Then make plans to connect with your partner in the next week to check in and encourage one another.

☐ **DO ONE THING TO SIMPLIFY YOUR LIFE.** Identify something you've given too much attention or desire to. Resolve to put it away—either mentally or literally, depending on what it is—for at least a week. When the week is over, think about how much priority that item or activity should really have in your life, and then decide what to do about it. If it's an item, you could even get rid of it—or find a person or organization to give it to.

☐ **TURN CONFLICTED RELATIONSHIPS AROUND.** Find that person who, like Euodia and Syntyche, you seem to have a lot of conflict with. Find a way you can be supportive of this person. How might they be "falling," and how can you be there to "catch" them? Remember them especially in prayer.

☐ **SUPPORT SOMEONE GOING THROUGH A HARD TIME.** This could be someone who is ill, has lost a loved one, lost a job, or, like Paul, is in jail. Visit or call them, and let them know you are praying for them (and then do it!). Listen to what their needs are, and see what you can do to meet those needs (or to connect them with someone who can).

☐ **CONTINUE TO WORK ON YOUR GROUP GROWTH GOAL.** If you chose this option last week, continue working toward your goal. How is the group doing? Continue to discuss ways you can reach out and include new people. And remember—this is a *group* goal.

Come back together as a group. Reread Philippians 4:6-7. Share prayer requests, and then pray for everyone's needs. Take time also to thank God for all he has done in your group's lives during this study.

Leader: If you haven't already, take some time to discuss what's next for the group. Will you stay together and work on another BibleSense book? Will you celebrate your time together with a party and be done? Or will you have a party, and *then* start another BibleSense book the following week?

Touch-base time:

Set a date, time, and place to get together with your touch-base partner in the next week.

Date _____

Time _____

Place _____

Taking It Home:

1. Touch base during the week with your weekly challenge partner to compare notes on how you're both doing with the goals you've set.

2. You may want to review this week's passage—or even watch the entire book of Philippians straight through on your DVD now that you've finished your study. (It takes about 16 minutes to watch the entire book.)

3. **I commit to touching my world this week by showing that Jesus is everything I need in the following ways:**

_____

_____

_____

_____

NOTES & ROLES

CONTENTS

LEADER NOTES

GROUP ROLES

GENERAL LEADER TIPS

1. Although these sessions are designed to require minimum advance preparation, try to read over each session ahead of time and watch the DVD chapter for that session. Highlight any questions you feel are especially important for your group to spend time on during the session.

2. Prior to the first session, watch the "Leading a BibleSense Session" overview on the DVD. You'll notice that this isn't your average Bible study. Food? Activities? Don't forget that Jesus used food and everyday items and experiences in *his* small group all the time. Jesus' disciples certainly weren't comfortable when he washed their feet (John 13:5-17), and were even a bit confused at first. Jesus reassured them, "You don't understand now what I am doing, but someday you will" (verse 7), and it turned out to be a powerful lesson that stayed with them the rest of their lives. It's our prayer that your group will have similar experiences.

3. Take the time to read the group roles on pages 82-84, and make sure all critical tasks and roles are covered for each session. The three roles you *absolutely need filled* for each session are Leader, Host, and Food Coordinator. These roles can be rotated around the group, if you like.

4. Discuss as a group how to handle child care—not only because it can be a sensitive subject but also to give your group an opportunity to begin working together *as* a group. See the Child Care Coordinator tips on page 92 for ideas on how to handle this important issue.

5. Don't be afraid to ask for volunteers. Who knows—they may want to commit to a role once they've tried it (and if it's available on a regular basis). However, give people the option of "no thanks" as well.

6. Every session will begin with a snack, so work closely with your Food Coordinator—he or she has a vital role in each session. If you need to, go ahead and ask for donations from your group for the snacks that are provided each week.

7. Always start on time. If you do this from Session 1, you'll avoid the group arriving and starting later as the study goes on.

8. Be ready and willing to pray at times other than the closing time. Start each session with prayer—let everyone know they're getting "down to business." Be open to other times where prayer is appropriate, such as when someone answers a question and ends up expressing pain or grief over a situation he or she is currently struggling with. Don't save it for the end—stop and pray right there and then. Your Prayer Coordinator can take the lead in these situations, if you like, but give him or her "permission" to do so.

9. Try not to have the first or last word on every question (or even most of them). Give everyone the opportunity to participate. At the same time, don't put anyone on the spot—remind group members that they can pass on any questions they're not comfortable answering.

10. Keep things on track. There are suggested time limits for each section. Encourage good discussion, but don't be afraid to "rope 'em back in." If you do decide to spend extra time on a question or activity, consider skipping or spending less time on a later question or activity so you can stay on schedule.

11. Don't let your group off the hook with the assignments in the "Touching Your World" section—this is when group members get to apply in a personal way what they have learned. Encourage group members to follow through on their assignments. You may even want to make it a point to ask how they did with their weekly challenges during snack time at the beginning of your next session.

12. Also note that the last weekly challenge in "Touching Your World" is often an outreach assignment that can be done either individually or as a group. Make sure that group members who take on these challenges are encouraged—and, if it's a group activity, organized. If your group has an Outreach Coordinator, let him or her take the lead here, and touch base regularly.

13. Lastly, research has shown that the single most important thing a leader can do for his or her group is to spend time in prayer for group members. Why not take a minute and pray for your group right now?

Session 1 Leader Notes

1. Read the General Leader Tips starting on page 73, if you haven't already. Take a peek at the tips for other group roles as well (pages 85-92).

2. Make sure everyone has a BibleSense book and DVD. Have the group pass around their books to record contact information (page 7) before or during "Taste and See" or at the end of the session.

3. If this is the first time you're meeting as a group, you may want to take a few minutes before your session to lay down some ground rules. Here are three simple ones:
   - Don't say anything that will embarrass anyone or violate someone's trust.
   - Likewise, anything shared in the group *stays* in the group, unless the person sharing it says otherwise.
   - No one has to answer a question he or she is uncomfortable answering.

4. Take time to review the group roles on pages 82-84 before you get together, and be ready to discuss them at the end of your session. Assign as many roles as you can, but don't pressure anyone to take on something he or she doesn't want to or isn't yet sure about.

5. For this session, you're responsible for the items in the Supplies list on page 8. You'll want to assign the Supplies list for future sessions; the Host is the most sensible choice to handle this responsibility, or it can be rotated around the group.

6. Unless you're ahead of the game and already have a Food Coordinator, you're responsible for the snack for this first session. You'll want to make sure you have a Food Coordinator for future sessions, but for this session, be sure to review the Food Coordinator assignment on page 85.

7. See the Extra Impact assignment at the end of your session, on page 17, and decide in advance whether this is something you'll want to do.

8. Before you dismiss this first session, make a special point to remind group members of the importance of following through on the weekly challenge each of them have committed to in the "Touching Your World" section.

Session 2 Leader Notes

1. If new people join the group this session, use part of the "Taste and See" time to ask them to introduce themselves to the group, and have the group pass around their books to record contact information (page 7). Give a brief summary of the points covered in Session 1.

2. If you told the group that you'd be following up to see how they did with their Touching Your World commitments, be sure to do it. This is an opportunity to establish an environment of accountability. You could use part of the "Taste and See" time to accomplish this. However, also be prepared to share how you did with your *own* commitment from the first session.

3. Take special note of the sensory experience in the "Digging Into Scripture" section. Before the session, you may want to think of an activity to do while your group's holding hands.

4. For the closing prayer time, ask for volunteers to pray for the requests that were shared. You may want to ask the Prayer Coordinator, if you have one, to lead the prayer time. If you do, ask in advance. Also, if your group has decided to use a prayer list, make sure you use it during your prayer time.

Session 3 Leader Notes

1. Congratulations! You're halfway through this study. It's time for a checkup: How's the group going? What's worked well so far? What might you consider changing as you approach the remaining sessions?

2. On that note, you may find it helpful to make some notes right after this session to help you evaluate how things are going. Ask yourself, "Did everyone participate?" and "Is there anyone I need to make a special effort to follow up with before the next session?"

3. Remember the importance of starting and ending on time, and remind your group of it, too, if you need to.

4. Your Food Coordinator will have two snacks for your group. The second snack is meant to be a surprise. Help him or her keep the surprise.

5. Look over the Supplies list. Make sure the bowls, rocks, pitchers of water, and bath towels are set out on a table in your meeting area before the group arrives.

6. If there are still group roles available, discuss them with your group again. Remember, God has created each member of your group for a different purpose. As group members take on roles, they'll feel more connected to the group and will even come to feel more comfortable doing what they're not sure they want to volunteer for right now.

Session 4 Leader Notes

1. See the Extra Impact assignment on page 41. Think about whether you'll do this as a group, and if so, who would be a good candidate to compile your group's recipes. If you choose to do this, contact group members in advance so they can locate their recipes. Make sure the index cards in the Supplies list are set out before the group arrives.

2. Include a time of prayer for the missionaries your church or small group supports. If possible, contact one or more of those missionaries to gather information for the group. Ask them to send you prayer requests and praises. If you can't get a response in time for this session, forward messages to your group when you get them, and ask group members to join you in regular prayer for these people. If your group has a Prayer Coordinator, pass this idea on to him or her.

3. Consider writing notes of thanks and encouragement to group members this week. Thank them for their commitment and contribution to the group, and let them know you're praying for them. (In fact, make a point of praying for them as you write their notes.) If your group has an Inreach Coordinator, encourage him or her to take on this task.

Session 5 Leader Notes

1. See the "Digging Into Scripture" section on page 55. If there's a particularly strong reader in your group, ask him or her in advance to be your reader for this passage.

2. Also, take note of the "Set a goal for your group" option in the "Touching Your World" section. Discuss ideas with your Outreach Coordinator—and other group members as well—before your group meets again.

3. This would be a good time to start thinking about how you're going to celebrate finishing this study. Will you do something next week or have a party the week after? Be ready to discuss it with the group this session.

Session 6 Leader Notes

1. Since this is your group's last session in this book, make sure you have a plan for next week...and beyond.

2. What did your group decide last week? Are you having a party? Are you going directly on to another BibleSense study? Finalize your plans.

3. As part of the final session of this study, you may want to consider having people share, either during the "Taste and See" section or at the end of your session, what this study or group has meant to them. You could also incorporate this into the beginning of your prayer time.

4. A reminder for your "Digging Into Scripture" sensory experience: If someone's in danger of not being caught due to height or weight or is unable or uncomfortable doing this physical activity, let him or her "take a pass."

5. Here's another suggestion for making the closing prayer time for this last session special: Have the group form a prayer circle. Then have each person or couple, if comfortable doing so, take a turn standing or kneeling in the middle of the circle while the group prays specifically for them. Your Prayer Coordinator is a good candidate to lead this time.

GROUP ROLES

ROLE DESCRIPTIONS

Review the group roles that follow.

We have provided multiple roles to encourage maximum participation. At minimum, there are three roles that we recommend be filled for every session— Leader, Food Coordinator, and Host. These particular roles can also be rotated around the group if you like. Other roles (Outreach and Inreach Coordinators, especially) are best handled by one person, as they involve tasks that may take more than one week to accomplish. It's *your* group—you decide what works best. What's most important is that you work together in deciding.

Not everyone will want to take on a role, so no pressure. But as you come to own a role in your group, you'll feel more connected. You'll even become more comfortable with that role you're not so sure you want to volunteer for right now.

Read through the following roles together, and write in each volunteer's name after his or her role in your book so everyone remembers who's who (and what roles may still be available):

LEADER _____.

Your session Leader will facilitate each session, keeping discussions and activities on track. If a role hasn't yet been filled or the person who normally has a certain role misses a session, the session Leader will also make sure that all tasks and supplies are covered.

FOOD COORDINATOR _____.

The Food Coordinator will oversee the snacks for each group meeting. This role not only builds the fellowship of the group, but it is an especially important role for this particular study, since specific snacks are assigned for each session and are used to lead group members into the meaning of each session.

HOST _____.

Your Host will open up his or her home and help group members and visitors feel *at* home. It sounds simple enough, but the gift of hospitality is critical to your group. If group members don't feel welcome, chances are they won't stay group members for long. Your Host should also be responsible for supplying—or locating someone who *can* supply—the items in the Supplies list at the beginning of each session. (They're usually common household items, so don't panic.)

OUTREACH COORDINATOR _____.

Different sessions often highlight different ways to reach out—sharing the Word, extending personal invitations to others to come to your group, or participating in service projects where your group meets the needs of those in your neighborhood or community. Your Outreach Coordinator will champion and coordinate those efforts to reach outside of your group.

GROUP CARE ("INREACH") COORDINATOR _____

_____. Everyone needs a pat on the back once in a while. Therefore, every group also needs a good Inreach Coordinator— someone who oversees caring for the personal needs of group members. That might involve coordinating meals for group members who are sick, making contact with those who have missed a session, arranging for birthday/anniversary celebrations for group members, or sending "just thinking of you" notes.

PRAYER COORDINATOR _____.

Your Prayer Coordinator will record and circulate prayer requests to the rest of the group during the week, as well as channel any urgent prayer requests to the group that may come up during the week. He or she may also be asked to lead the group in prayer at the close of a session.

SUBGROUP LEADER(S) _____

_____.

To maximize participation and also to have enough time to work through the session, at various points we recommend breaking into smaller subgroups of three or four. Therefore, you'll also need Subgroup Leaders. This is also a great opportunity to develop leaders within the group (who could possibly lead new groups in the future).

CHILD CARE COORDINATOR _____.

Your Child Care Coordinator will make arrangements to ensure that children are cared for while their parents meet, either at the Host's house or at some other agreed-upon location(s). Depending on the makeup of your group, this could be a make-or-break role in ensuring you have a healthy group.

Again, if you don't have volunteers for every role (aside from Leader, Food Coordinator, and Host), that's OK. You may need to think about it first or become more comfortable before making a commitment. What's important is that once you commit to a role, you keep that commitment. If you know you'll miss a session, give the session Leader as much advance notice as possible so your role can be covered.

Whether you volunteer for a role now or want to think things over, take time before the next session to look over the "Group Role Tips" section that begins on the following page. You'll find plenty of useful ideas that will help your group and your role in it (or the role you're considering) to be the best it can be.

GROUP ROLE TIPS

FOOD COORDINATOR

1. Sometimes your snack will be a surprise to the rest of the group. Be sure to work closely with your Leader and Host so the timing of your snacks helps each session be the best it can be.

2. You may also need to arrive a few minutes early to set up the surprise. Set up a time with the Host for your arrival before the meeting.

FOOD COORDINATOR ASSIGNMENTS AND IDEAS
Session 1
Your first snack as a group will be "prison food." Set out the following for your guests:

- Plain white or flat bread
- Water

Be sure to have "real" snacks to put out for your group a little later, but not before they've had a chance to "enjoy" this first snack and discuss the questions in the "Taste and See" section of this session.

Session 2
This week, prepare a pie—or more than one pie if your group has more than eight people. But make sure you *don't* slice the pie(s) beforehand! Read through the "Taste and See" section to find out why.

Session 3
This week's snack has two courses.

- Course One is chocolate-covered strawberries and sparkling grape juice or cider. (If these aren't available, it's OK to substitute—but the idea here is to provide a "luxurious" snack.)
- Course Two should be easier—heated plain beef or chicken broth. Use foam cups to serve this course, so no one's hands are burned by the hot broth.

Keep this second course a secret from the rest of the group, as best you can, until it's time to serve it.

Session 4

Have a favorite family recipe (of your own choice) prepared for your group. But it can't be a "secret recipe"—because you'll also pass out recipe cards for the dish. Be sure to make one recipe card for each member of your group, and have a few extras available in case you have visitors.

Also, look now at your instructions for *next* week—you'll probably want to get an early jump on things.

Session 5

Contact group members several days before this session or talk with them after the end of Session 4. Ask each person what dessert *he or she* would like for the next session—with the provision that it's something that can be easily purchased at the store. Arrange to get one serving of each of those desserts, and bring them to this session.

Don't be afraid to ask for donations if you need them. Also, keep an extra snack handy in case you have guests this week.

Session 6

For this session, your only "official" snack is coffee and tea. Give your group members a variety of choices, and include some decaffeinated teas and coffee among your choices. Bring some other snacks of your own choice as well, but save them for after your "coffee time."

And thank you for all your work in making this a successful study!

HOST

1. Before your group gets together, make sure the environment for your session is just right. Is the temperature in your home or meeting place comfortable? Is there enough lighting? Are there enough chairs for everyone? Can they be arranged in a way that everyone's included? Is your bathroom clean and "stocked"? Your home doesn't need to win any awards—just don't let anything be a distraction from your time together.

2. Once your session has started, do what you can to keep it from being interrupted. When possible, don't answer the phone. Ask people to turn off their cell phones or pagers, if necessary. If your phone number is an emergency contact for someone in the group, designate a specific person to answer the phone, so your session can continue to run smoothly.

3. If you're responsible for the supplies for your study, be sure to read through the Supplies list before each session. If there's any difficulty in supplying any of the materials, let your Leader know or contact someone else in the group who you know has them. The items required for each session are usually common household items, so most weeks this will be pretty easy. Make sure everything's set up before the group arrives.

4. Be sure to also check out what the Food Coordinator's got planned each week. Sometimes the snack is a surprise, so he or she may need your help in *keeping* it a surprise from the rest of the group. Your Food Coordinator may also need to arrive a few minutes early to set up, so be sure to work out a time for his or her arrival before the meeting.

5. And, of course, make your guests feel welcome. That's your number-one priority as Host. Greet group members at the door, and make them feel at home from the moment they enter. Spend a few minutes talking with them after your session—let them know you see them as people and not just "group members." Thank them for coming as they leave.

OUTREACH COORDINATOR

1. Don't forget: New people are the lifeblood of a group. They will keep things from getting stale and will keep your group outwardly focused—as it should be. Encourage the group to invite others.

2. Don't overlook the power of a personal invitation—even to those who don't know Jesus. Invite people from work or your neighborhood to your group, and encourage other group members to do the same.

3. Take special note of the "Touching Your World" section at the end of each session. The last weekly challenge is often an outreach assignment that can be done either individually or as a group. Be sure to encourage and follow up with group members who take on these challenges.

4. If group members choose an outreach option for their weekly challenge, use part of your closing time together to ask God for help in selecting the right service opportunity and that God would bless your group's efforts. Then spend some time afterward discussing what you'll do next.

5. Consider having an event before you begin your BibleSense study (or after you finish it). Give a "no obligation" invite to Christians and non-Christians alike, just to have the opportunity to meet the others in your group. Do mention, however, what the group will be studying next, so they have an opportunity to consider joining you for your next study. Speak with your Leader before making any plans, however.

6. As part of your personal prayer time, pray that God would bring new people to the group. Make this a regular part of your group's prayer time as well.

GROUP CARE ("INREACH") COORDINATOR

1. Make it a point to find out more about your group members each week. You should be doing this as a group member, but in your role as Inreach Coordinator, you'll have additional opportunities to use what you learn to better care for those in your group.

2. If a group member has special needs, be sure to contact him or her during the week. If it's something the group can help with, get permission first, and then bring the rest of the group into this ministry opportunity.

3. Find out the special dates in your group members' lives, such as birthdays or anniversaries. Make or bring cards for other group members to sign in advance.

4. If someone in your group is sick, has a baby, or faces some other kind of emergency, you may want to coordinate meals for that person with the rest of the group.

PRAYER COORDINATOR

1. Pray for your group throughout the week, and encourage group members to pray for one another. Keep a prayer list, and try to send out prayer reminders after each session.

2. Be sure to keep your group up to date on any current or earlier prayer requests. Pass on "praise reports" when you have them. Remind them that God not only hears, but *answers* prayer.

3. Remember that the role is called Prayer *Coordinator,* not "Official Pray-er for the Group" (whether that's what your group would prefer or not). At the same time, some members of your group may be uncomfortable praying aloud. If there are several people in your group who don't mind praying, one person could open your prayer time and another close it, allowing others to add prayers in between. Give everyone who wants to pray the opportunity to do so.

4. Prayers don't have to be complex, and probably shouldn't be. Jesus himself said, "When you pray, don't babble on and on as people of other religions do. They think their prayers are answered merely by repeating their words again and again" (Matthew 6:7).

5. If some group members are intimidated by prayer, begin prayer time by inviting group members to complete a sentence as he or she prays. For example, ask everyone to finish the following: "Lord, I want to thank you for..."

6. Don't overlook the power of silent prayer. Don't automatically fill "dead spaces" in your prayer time—God may be trying to do that by speaking into that silence. You might even consider closing a session with a time of silent prayer.

SUBGROUP LEADER(S)

1. These sessions are designed to require a minimum of preparation. Nonetheless, be sure to read over each session and watch the DVD in advance to get comfortable with those sections where you may be responsible for leading a subgroup discussion. Highlight any questions you think are important for your subgroup to spend time on for next session.

2. Try not to have the first or last word on every question (or even most of them). Give everyone the opportunity to participate. At the same time, don't put anyone on the spot—let subgroup members know they can pass on any question they're not comfortable answering.

3. Keep your subgroup time on track. There are suggested time limits for each section. Encourage good discussion, but don't be afraid to "rope 'em back in." If you do decide to spend extra time on a question or activity, consider skipping or spending less time on a later question or activity so you can stay on schedule.

CHILD CARE COORDINATOR

There are several ways you can approach the important issue of child care. Discuss as a group which alternative(s) you'll use:

1. The easiest approach may be for group members to each make their own child care arrangements. Some might prefer this; others may not be able to afford it on their own. If a parent or couple needs financial assistance, see if someone else in the group can help out in this area.

2. If your meeting area is conducive to it, have everyone bring their children to the meeting, and have on-site child care available so parents can pay on a child-by-child basis.

> **Important:** It is wise to prescreen any potential child care worker—paid or volunteer—who is watching children as part of a church-sanctioned activity (including a home Bible study). Your church may already have a screening process in place that can be utilized for your group. If not, Group's Church Volunteer Central network (www.churchvolunteercentral .com) is a great resource, containing ready-made background-check and parental-consent forms as well as articles and other online resources.

3. If most or all of your group members have young children, you could also consider rotating child care responsibilities around the group rather than paying someone else.

4. If there are members in your group with older children who are mature enough to watch the younger children, pay them to handle your child care. Maybe they can even do their own lesson. If so, Group offers a number of great materials for children of all ages—go to www.group.com to find out more.

5. Check to see if the youth group at your church would be interested in providing child care as a fund-raiser.